101 FRUGAL LIVING TIPS

SPEND LESS AND SAVE MORE

Kevin C. Hill

Introduction

I want to thank you and congratulate you for downloading the book, *"101 FRUGAL LIVING TIPS: SPEND LESS AND SAVE MORE"*.

This book contains proven steps and strategies on how to Spend less money and save more .

Our first book "Frugal Living", focuses more on the mindset of an individual who lives a frugal lifestyle. I believe that an individual that lives a frugal lifestyle is not necessarily a cheap person, but a person who values and respects money. Some of the most successful people in the world as far as finances are concerned are actually frugal individuals. Don't be fooled by what you see on television, people foolishly wasting money on things that they don't need and flashing money around. These people who throw their money around and have no respect for it, typically lose their money in a short period of time. Many financially successful people got to where they are financially because they were very intelligent and frugal with their money. Many people ask for more money, but they don't know how to manage the money that they are currently making. Change your thinking change your life!

With 101 frugal living tips, we want to share with you 101 ways that you can actually save money and live a more frugal lifestyle. So many people asked for a book with more ideas on living a frugal lifestyle and now you have it. With the tips in this book, you will learn how to save more money and be able to reinvest that money which will help you grow financially. Most of the things that we share you are probably doing anyway, we will just share you a better way to do it.

For some of you you, these tips may be brand new to you. You may have come from an environment where people were wasteful with money and always struggle in life because of it. I applaud you for taking initiative on changing things. The definition of insanity is doing the same thing over and over and expecting a different result. Some of the greatest information that you can find is actually in books. Every time I read a book if I can walk away with at least one thing, I've got my money's worth and more from that book. One of the key things that you want to do after reading this book is to take action.   The average person learns great ideas and great tips, but they don't take action on them. If you want to step out of the average lane into the fast lane of success, whatever you learn of value implement it as quickly as possible.

Thanks again for downloading this book, I hope you enjoy it!

1: Save loose change

Many people overlook loose change, for some reason it gets overlooked. Take all of your loose change put it in a jar or bag. Take it to the bank and put it in a savings.

2: Do you know how much your spending

Do you have any idea what you are spending, most people don't. it is very important to know what's coming in and also what is going out as far as your money is concerned. If you don't know your number you will never be able to grow your number. The average person has not been taught how to manage their money properly and this is why most people struggle financially. Invest in books, audio tapes, and live events that will teach you how to manage your money properly.

3: Never purchase expensive items on impulse

Many bad decisions are made because people have a tendency of buying on impulse. If you think about it, how many times have you bought something off of impulse and then later had buyer's remorse? For now on before purchasing anything take at least 20 seconds to ask yourself "what I'm about to buy, do I really need it?" I think you will find most of the time that you don't necessarily need what you're about to buy.

4: Practice preventative dental care

You can save yourself some serious money by being prevented with your dental care. If you are not taking care of your teeth it can become very expensive down the line for you. Make sure to floss and brush your teeth multiple times a day along with your regular dentist visits.

5: Buy items online in bulk

When making purchases instead of going and buying one by one, get into a habit of buying in bulk. There are many wholesale membership businesses like BJ's and Sam's Club that sell many products from clothing, food, appliances and many more at a steep wholesale discount. Buying in bulk will save you time and money.

6: Buy coffee in bulk

Coffee can be very expensive habit, many people cannot start their day without their favorite brew. I heard it said somewhere that the average person drinks 3 to 5 cups of coffee per day. Some businesses actually sell their coffee for $5 a cup. If you do the math on this, that is some serious money being spent on a monthly basis. Now I don't think there's anything wrong with having your cup of coffee. I don't agree with giving it up completely on what you love to do. But buying it in bulk can give you a significant savings. If at all possible cutting down on some of your consumption a day will be a great savings as well.

7: Eat out less

How often do you order takeout or eat at restaurants per month. Again I don't think it's anything wrong with this but you want to do it in moderation. A couple going out to eat on average might spend about $50, and I think that's really conservative. A family will typically spend much more. That same $50 at a supermarket will stock your refrigerator for multiple meals.

8: Always shop for food with a list

Nowadays not many people use a list when shopping. If you talk to your mother or grandmother, preparing a list before you go to the supermarket was an automatic thing. Having a list is really helpful because you are going to the supermarket with a plan in mind. When you don't have a plan you will notice that you overspend and you also many times by duplicate things that you already have in your home.

9: Buy store brand medications

Many people don't realize this but many store brands actually use the same ingredients to make some medicines as big brand. You know what I mean, the ones we tend to call "name brand products". If you do your research on this you will find that cough medicines, aspirin and many others have the same ingredients. Buying the store brand in some cases you can save up to 50%

10: Never go to the supermarket when you are hungry

If you have ever went to the supermarket when you are hungry you know that it is very easy to buy things that you don't need. When you are hungry you want to eat everything in the store. Not going hungry will keep you focused on buying what you came to buy.

11: Only use your bank's ATM

Using ATMs outside of your bank's ATM in my opinion is ridiculous. I have never been a fan of paying for my own money. There is typically a fee of a few dollars to get cash from an ATM other than your bank's ATM. It may not seem like a huge cost but over time it can add up to a pretty huge amount. If you are someone who doesn't like to carry around cash, make sure to keep at least $40-$60 bucks in your wallet or pocket book just in case of emergency so that you don't waste money on ATM fees.

12: Make monthly credit card payments on time

Credit card companies make the bulk of their money from people being late on making their payments. Make your monthly credit card payments on time. The best thing to do is set it up automatic payment so that the payment is taken directly from your bank account. You now don't have to think about it. Eventually you want to get to a point of only making purchases on your credit card when you know you can pay it off in 30 days or less. There will be no interest charged to you when you pay your credit card off in less than 30 days. Be sure to keep track of your credit card statements when you pay it off early. I have noticed many times that the credit card company has tried to sneak in the interest fees even though I paid it off early. By noticing this I simply gave the company a call and they removed it right away. Always inspect what you expect!

13: Reduce credit card debt

How much do you have in credit card that right now? and how much are you paying in interest for that credit card that? this is why many times it's hard to get out of credit card debt because the interest fees are so high. Sometimes just calling up the credit card company and asking politely if they can lower your interest payments works. Another option is to apply for a zero interest credit card. I've seen zero interest credit cards for up to 24 months. That can be a significant savings on interest over 2 years, which will speed up the process of getting rid of debt and/or reducing debt.

14: Take fewer cab rides use Uber more

If you are someone who takes cab rides often you should seriously take a look into what you what Uber is doing. Uber connects you with qualified independent drivers, who have their own qualified vehicles. Because Uber has no employees and no vehicles they are able to tremendously cut cost with their driving services. There are other services like this that exist, but this one is my favorite.

15: Don't pay for space you don't need

If you are looking to buy a home or apartment, or you already have one or the other, don't waste money on space that you don't need. You can even consider renting out additional space in your home as an option to bring cash flow in as this well.

16: Live near your job or business

Living near your job or business can be really beneficial in a lot of ways. For one thing your commute would be shorter, and you probably wouldn't even have to use a vehicle depending on how close it is. Some people spend hours a day stuck in traffic, living close to your job or business would give you much more time and peace in your life.

17: Refinance your mortgage

With interest rates being at an all time low now is the best time to refinance your mortgage. I have seen situations where some people have cut their interest rate almost in half because of how low the rates are right now. leading to a tremendous savings on their mortgage. Take advantage!

18: Choose home repair contractors wisely

When using a contractor never go with the first estimate that you get. There are many websites now where you can have contractors come to your home and give you a free estimate to help you get the best savings possible. Compare between at least 5 different businesses if possible. With technology now there is no reason to ever pay full price anymore.

19: Weatherproof your home

Weatherproofing your home can save you a huge amount of money. If you have old drafty windows, there are different window treatments that you can actually buy that will significantly help you save on your heating and cooling bill. Go around your home and seal cracks with caulk around windows, doors and in different places in your home. Eventually upgrading to weather efficient windows is the way to go.

20: Use window coverings to block or let in sunshine

Using window coverings can be a good way to weatherproof your home and cut down on energy usage. In the summer window coverings can keep the sun out of your home which will keep it cooler. In the winter by opening up the coverings when the sun is out will actually help heat your.

21: Look for sales at discount outlets

There are so many discount outlets to choose from. Before making any purchases you should always go on different sites like eBay, Amazon etc. to compare prices. You can easily save 50% or more on different products.

22: Purchasing previously-used clothes

You can take advantage of huge savings by purchasing previously used clothing. You can find previously used clothing on eBay, consignment shops and other places as well. You can find many name brand products like Gucci, polo, Louis Vuitton and many more that are slightly used but in really good condition. Many wealthy people that purchase products like these are always looking to help others out. They understand that the more you give the more you will receive, so they give these products away to consignment shops. Whenever you get a chance stop by and take advantage of great deals.

23: Clean clothes inexpensively

Whether you are going to the cleaners to have your clothes cleaned, or cleaning your clothes in your home you can save money. Check around town at different cleaners in your area to see if you can save money. Maybe the savings won't be a much but it all adds up. keep in mind the proximity of the cleaners makes a difference in how much you pay as far as gas and time is concerned.

24: Lower cell phone bill

Look at your cell phone bill and see if there are some services that you can cut back on that are unnecessary. I was recently able to save $40 by cutting back on how much gigs I was paying for because I wasn't using them. Also occasionally call up your cell phone provider and see if there's any way that they can help you lower your bill. Sometimes things change with the company and you may be able to get lower rates and not even know it.

25: Cut back or give up cable

I know that cable television is a soft spot for people. If you review how often you are watching some of the premium channels you may be able to cut back and not even miss them. In some cases you probably could get rid of it totally and not miss it with some of the new technology available. Services like Netflix which is about $8 a month, google has something called chromecast which you can cast content from online to your television which is a one time cost of $30. hundreds of dollars a month can be saved here alone.

26: Move bank accounts to take advantage bonuses

Santander bank has a bonuses we're just by opening up a savings account they'll pay you $20 a month. Some banks give you higher interest as well, even though overall interest is very low through bank accounts. There are many other great promotions and deals out there make sure to look around.

27: Turn off the television when not using

I know this one is obvious but may not be obvious to everyone. When you leave the room or before you fall asleep turn the television off. No need to waste money on the television playing and you're not even watching it.

28: Cut down buying and start selling

The reason that most people are in debt is because they are buyers not sellers. As a nation we have become professional buyers. Have you noticed that most financially successful people sell something? Look through your home and find things that you are no longer using. Places like eBay and Amazon, you can sell items that you are not using and make money. This is a good way to start earning additional income.

29: Make your own gifts instead of buying from the store

Simple things like making your own gifts can save you a great amount of money. It's also pretty cool because it adds a personal touch to your gift. Things like cookies, cakes, cupcakes, soap are a few examples.

30: Invite your friends over instead of going out

Have game night and invite friends over, they can also bring a dish with them instead of going out.

31: Repair clothing

Sewing is a skill that is not used much anymore. Sometimes people get rid of a shirt just because it lost its button. Or maybe your stitching comes out off your pants, and now you take them to the cleaners to get tailoring done and have to pay out of pocket. Being able to do small jobs like this can save you time and money. If you have never sewn before check out some YouTube videos on the topic, you'll be surprised at how simple small sewing jobs are.

32: Cut cost on expensive entertainment for children

Some of the entertainment that we are doing for our children is really not for our children, it's actually for us. Some of the things that my family has done for our kids as far as entertainment at an early age, the kids cannot even remember. I believe the most important things with kids that they will always remember is time that you spend with them. Many times you can get as much from taking your child to the park or maybe to the zoo as you would going out of state.

33: Clean your closets

Take some time and clean out your closets. This will not only help your sanity, but also many times you will find duplicates as well. When there's so much clutter around your home many times you do not realize that you're going out to buy things that you already have in your home. It would be healthier for you mentally as well.

34: Learn how to cook

If you want to save yourself a tremendous amount of money and also eat more healthier, you should absolutely learn how to cook. You could take the money from one night of going to a restaurant and use it to go shopping and possibly be able to feed yourself for a week or more. Cooking is also fun and therapeutic as well.

35: Quit smoking

Do you know that the average smoker spends about $1500 to $3,000 a year in cigarettes. I know that smoking is an addiction and it is a very tough habit for many people to break. Breaking the habit can be better on your wallet and your health.

36: Take advantage of yard sales

At yard sales you can find great deals on things that you may not be able to find anywhere else. You can also resell these items on eBay and Amazon as well.

37: Convert to energy efficient appliances

Many times we think that we are saving money by using old appliances and electronics. but technology has changed so much that you could be losing a lot of money by not upgrading. Compare old appliances that you currently have to newer energy efficient appliances.

38: Turn off the lights

When you leave all the rooms in your home make sure to turn the lights off. Not a big savings here, but again will add up over time. It's also promotes good habits.

39: Buy quality things

Buying quality is really important. When buying cheap things you end up having to buy them over and over again. So you defeat the purpose of saving money. Many times you end up spending more money then the product that you thought was expensive in the first place. In most cases the reason that they are cheap is because they are not made well. Quality things are typically made of the best materials available so that they last longer. Now don't confuse the price with quality, you should always be looking for a good deal. Just make sure that it is good quality.

40: Install smart thermostat

Just like the smartphone now we have smart thermostats. you can now control the temperature of your home from anywhere around the world right from your cell phone or computer. You no longer have to leave the heating or cooling system on to keep the room at a comfortable temperature when you arrive. You can now set the date and time that you will arrive and the smart thermostat will prepare the room for you.

41: Stay away from spending when stressed

Some people have a bad habit of shopping when they are stressed. This habit can become very expensive. If you are stressed look into other things that you can do besides shopping to relieve stress. Maybe cooking, listening to music, or exercising.

42: Get rid of any club memberships that you are not using

Go to your bank account and see what memberships you are paying for that you are not using. Sometimes you will be surprised to find memberships that you didn't realize were monthly memberships on your account. If you are not using them get rid of them immediately.

43: Buy used when it makes sense

In some situations it makes sense to buy used instead of buying brand new. For example, you can buy electronics refurbished and you would not be able to tell the difference. With refurbished electronics the company is giving the product a total overhaul making it like new.

44: Do holiday shopping after the holidays

There are so many tremendous deals and sales right after the holidays. Prices are significantly slashed. Also take advantage of big shopping days like black friday and cyber Monday. Just remember to always use a list so that you don't unnecessarily overspend.

45: Buy generic brands of items instead

Now I don't like to call them generic brands but I'm using this because I know that you'll understand right away what I'm talking about. Generic can make it sound like it's cheap, and many times this is the furthest thing from the truth. In many cases the so-called generic brands are actually owned by the same companies that you see advertised on television. I found this out from a friend that works in the grocery industry. Because we see so much advertising all day long between television and product placement we believe that certain products are the best. Try some of these products you'll be blown away at some of the quality. Some of them are even better then the big brands.

46: Cut down on trips to the mall

I don't know if you're like me but for some reason going to the mall you end up spending money that you didn't plan to spend. If this is a problem for you as well cut down on your trips to the mall.

47: Fix things around your home yourself

If you own your home you already know that things eventually break. I have a toilet issue right now as we speak. It will cost me $25 to buy the parts to fix it, and probably about an hour of my time. If I was to pay someone to fix the same problem it will cost me $400. There's many things around your home that are not too difficult to fix. If you are handy you can save a lot of money by doing smaller jobs on your own. If you are not handy buy a Home Depot has a do it yourself book. It is very helpful for making home repairs.

48: Purchase a deep freezer

Purchasing a deep freezer is one of the best purchases that you can make. We spoke earlier about buying food in bulk. If you don't have a deep freezer it would be difficult to buy food in bulk. Having a deep freezer will cut down on trips and save you money on food.

49: Keep tire inflate when necessary

Do you know that you can improve your gas mileage up to 3.3% by keeping your tires inflated to the recommended pressure? Look in your car manual and and find out what the the recommended pressure is. Some cars will give you an alert when it drops below that mark.

50: Cut your own hair

If you have a simple hairstyle or cut, do your own hair. I believe that appearance is very important. if you are not good at cutting your hair I would not necessarily do it. But if it is something that you can manage, you can save a great deal by doing your own hair.

51: Buy a crock pot

A crockpot can save you time and money. Before going to work you can actually make a meal in a crock pot and it will cook for the whole day. It's almost like having a chef helping you out while you're at work or busy. When you get home you have a meal waiting on you. Also you can make enough they can last you for multiple days saving you more time and money.

52: Don't speed

Speeding while driving cannot only cost you money as far as tickets are concerned, but they can also cost you money by wasting gas. Slow down a bit!

53: Negotiate everything

Before making any purchases of any kind, whether business or personal, you want to get into a habit of asking "is that the best that you can do?" Many times by asking this simple question you will get major discounts. Don't be afraid to walk away if you do not get a discount. There is so much competition right now as far as business somebody will give you the price that you're looking for.

54: Exercise at home

If you like the gym keep your membership. If you are like most people who have a gym membership but don't use it, that's an expense that you can cut. There are many great exercise programs on video that is almost like having a personal trainer in your home. There are also many fat burning exercises like burpees, pull ups and others that you can do right from the comfort of your home.

55: Take public transportation

If you drive your car to work everyday replacing some of those days by driving public transportation may make sense for you.

56: Dry your clothes on a clothesline

This one is a little old school but saves money. If you have a basement or space outside, set up a clothesline and let clothes air dry instead of using the dryer.

57: Make your own snacks

How much money do you think you spend a month at the vending machine at work? Use sandwich bags and pack your snacks at home.

58: Buy a filter instead of bottled water

You may not remember this but at one time water was free. Over the years spring water has become a hot commodity and for many good reasons. Simply purchase a filter for your home and start saving money right away.

59: Listen to music for free on Spotify and Pandora

Technology has really changed the way that things are now being done. Instead of downloading music and paying for it, you can now download music for free on apps like Spotify and Pandora.

60: Brush and floss your teeth everyday

This is a simple one that we all know we should be doing multiple times a day. Not being proactive and taking care of your teeth can cost a lot of money. Be sure to brush your teeth at least twice a day and floss before going to bed.

61: Explore your city instead of taking an out of state vacation

How well do you know your city? Recently my family and I took a tour of our city, it was the first time that I've ever did this. I had no idea how many great things were going on in my city that I had lived in most of my life. Sometimes we are so infatuated for taking a vacation out of state that we may be missing something beautiful right at home. If you want to have that vacation feel, you can also rent a condo or home, and cut your costs dramatically because you won't be spending money on flights. You also won't spin most of your time traveling!.

62: Use WiFi when you can to conserve data on your smartphone

There was a time when Wi-Fi wasn't free, You had to pay for it by the minute. Now just about anywhere you go you can get free Wi-Fi. so remember to conserve data just by simply putting your phone on Wi-Fi setting when you're in an area that has it. Also if you have a tablet, I don't see any sense in paying for online service when you have Wi-Fi in most places.

63: Use apps like GasBuddy.com to find cheapest gas

In the past, to find out about a gas station that had cheap gas you either had to stumble upon it or be referred by someone. Now the only thing you have to do is download an app like gasbuddy.com that will show you the cheapest gas within the vicinity that you're in.

64: Consider a Condos or a vacation rental home instead of a hotel

Renting a home or condo when you are on vacation is really cost effective especially if you have a family. You will have a full kitchen that can help you save money on food. Also many times is actually less expensive to rent. These are just a few of the bonuses.

65: Use vinegar to clean your home

Vinegar is great to have in your cleaning arsenal. It's great for lifting stains, freshening laundry, cleaning windows, and so many other great uses as well.

66: Grow your own vegetables

Growing your own vegetables is not only great for saving you money, but also a healthy way to eat your vegetables as well.

67: Carpool

If you have some friends or family members that are going in the same direction and you are living near each other, every now and then pull together and carpool. depending on the size of the car if you have 5 to 8 people you can put your money together for gas and save money. It can also be a lot of fun!

68: Cut back on water usage

When you are doing things like washing your hair or washing your car for example, turn the water off in between when you are not using it. More water is probably wasted then used in situations like this.

69: Make your own cleaning supplies

Today people are more health conscious than ever. We are starting to realize that many chemicals that are in different products like home cleaners may be hazardous to our health. Therefore making your own cleaning supplies from things like baking soda, lemon juice, vinegar, rubbing alcohol and many others natural products will help you live a healthier lifestyle and save money.

70: Switch to energy efficient lighting

Switching to energy efficient light bulbs will not be a huge savings, maybe a few dollars per light bulb per year. Remember overtime is where your savings will be.

80: Bring your own bags to the grocery store

Most supermarkets charge you to buy shopping bags. By simply bringing your own bags you can save yourself money.

81: Eat leftovers

When I was a child leftovers were part of daily life. Nowadays I don't hear about people eating leftovers as much. You don't have to just eat regular leftovers, you can spice them up as well. For example there is so many things that you can do with leftover chicken. Chicken soup, chicken sandwich etc. Have fun with it, see how many meals you can come up with from 1 dish.

82: Cook larger amounts of food

Instead of cooking one meal at a time, get into a habit of cooking larger meals. This can save you time and money, you could possibly have 3-5 meals by just cooking a larger amount of food. This is really important nowadays because in many families both parents are working and don't have a lot of time. You can also freeze the food to make it last longer.

83: Eat from your stocked pantry

Make it a night of family fun and be creative by cooking only from the pantry. Children get really excited about this and it's something that the family can have fun with.

84: Make your own baby food

Making your own baby food will not only help you save money, but it is also healthier for your baby as well.

85: Ride your bike

Riding your bike more can help you save money on gas and also help you become healthier as well.

86: Fill up your gas tank when it's half empty

Many people don't realize it but when you run your gas empty before filling up you actually burn gas faster. Get into a habit of refilling when your tank is half empty.

87: Unplug every electrical devices at night

When you leave electronic devices plugged in but turned off they still use a small amount of electricity. Get into a habit of unplugging all of them before you go to sleep.

88: Use a fan more

When possible give the central air and air conditioners a break. The good ol box fan or ceiling fan every now and then will help save money.

89: Use rechargeable batteries

For toys & electronics use rechargeable batteries. These cost a little bit more than regular batteries, but you can get much longer use out of them.

90: Look for free samples

There are many companies that are looking to give their products away for free. Just go online and in the search engine put in free samples, and also check for free samples of your favorite products.

91: Use leftover water for plants

It may sound disgusting to use leftover water from washing your hair and showers, but your plants will love it. This will save you money on your water bill.

92: Take advantage of points for hotels and airlines

If you travel a lot be sure to set yourself up to get points from hotel and airline use. Some airlines and hotels have a credit card system setup where they'll keep points while you're traveling and booking hotels. This is a good way to occasionally get free flights and free hotel stays.

93: Share your meal when you go out to dinner

This is not something you have to do all the time, but if you know you're going to a restaurant that serves a lot of food why not share the meal. My wife almost never finishes a meal when we go out to eat we share majority of the time and are both usually full.

94: Do your own landscaping

Instead of paying someone to cut your grass, invest in a lawn mower and trimmer and save money by doing it yourself.

95: Have a garage sale

If you're looking to make some extra money have a garage sale. This is also great to remove clutter from your home.

96: Use cash more often

Sometimes when using credit cards you don't realize how much money you are actually spending. Credit cards can sometimes make you feel like you have more money than what you have. When possible , use cash instead of credit. It can be cheaper to use your cash as well.

97: Get off promotional email list

As promotional emails are sent to you take yourself off. When you know you are in the market to make a purchase then go ahead and get the information on that product. The only thing that being on a promotional list does is put you in a position sometimes to spend money unnecessarily.

98: Combine errands to cut down on gas

Before going out to run your errands check around with some of your friends to see if you can carpool to run your errands together. This will help cut gas cost.

99: Throw catalogues away when they come in the mail

There is a reason why companies send catalogs to your home on a consistent basis. This is because companies know that there's a great chance that you will open them up and then open up your checkbook. As I stated earlier I don't think there's anything wrong with purchasing things that you want occasionally, but most people buy emotionally not logically. Many times the things that you purchase you do not need them, you just got emotionally excited about it.

100: Work from home a few days a week if possible

If you are in good standings with your boss ask if it's possible if you could work a few days from home if your job permit sit. If this is possible you could save a serious amount of money by not having to drive back and forth to work.

101: When there is a great deal on things you use often stockpile it

We all come across really good sales every now and then. If you know that the item is something that you constantly use get into a habit of stockpiling the it so that you save more money.

102: Stop drinking soda

Soda is really not good for you and has a ton of sugar in it. Cut back on soda or get or get rid of it altogether and replace it with water.

103: Use tea bags more than once

Depending on the kind of tea that you are drinking you should be able to get more than one cup of tea from one bag .

104: Download coupon apps

There are many different coupon apps that you can now use to save money on anything that you can think of. Download apps right onto your smartphone to start saving right away.

105: Become a preferred customer at your supermarket

If you are not a preferred customer at your supermarket become one right away. By becoming a preferred customer you will sign up and get a key fob. You'll be in the supermarket system to get savings on different sales.

106: Reinvest savings

From using these tips you will be able to save more money. The last thing you want to do is take your savings and spend it on liabilities only. Liabilities are things that take money out of your pocket. You want to reinvest your savings into things that will put money back into your pocket which are called assets.

107: Swap babysitting with friends and family

If you have friends and family members with children swap babysitting to save money.

108: Make your own popsicles and ice cream for kids

We all know that kids love ice cream and popsicles. Simply use an ice cube tray or take a few dollars and buy popsicle and ice cream holders. You can now use juice in your home to make popsicles.

109: Reverse ceiling fans

Reversing ceiling fans is a real simple way to help better heat your room with less heat. This will actually distribute heat throughout the room more evenly. Also close vents in rooms that are not being used, this will cut down on energy as well.

110: Monitor your bank account on a daily basis

You should check your bank accounts on a daily basis. After reading this book never let a day go past without taking a look at your bank account and your finances at least for a few minutes a day. This is what separates successful people from unsuccessful people when it comes to your finances. How can you ever change or grow your finances if you have no idea what's coming in and what's going out. Take control of your finances!

Conclusion

Thank you again for downloading this book!

I hope this book was able to help you to spend less and save more money. Remember to take action on what you have learned in this book right away.

The next step is to take MASSIVE ACTION!!!

Finally, if you enjoyed this book, then I'd like to ask you for a favor, would you be kind enough to leave a review for this book on Amazon? It'd be greatly appreciated!

Click here to leave a review for this book on Amazon!

Thank you and good luck!

Click here to check out the rest of (MONEY MANAGEMENT TIPS) on Amazon.

Chapter 1

Why is it important to better manage your money

It is very important to learn the skill of money management. I heard it said that money isn't everything, but it ranks right up there with oxygen. Money has an impact in just about every area of our lives. Unfortunately there isn't a course in school on the topic. The most that you may learn in school is how to balance a checkbook if you're fortunate. This is probably the reason why majority of the population has zero in savings. Majority of the population is 1-2 paychecks away from literally being on the street. It doesn't take a rocket scientist to realize that what most of us have learned about money just isn't working.

It's not how much you make but how much you keep

The thing that I hear often is people saying "I need to make more money." Don't get me wrong, I think everyone would like to increase their net worth. But I also think the reason that most people want to make more money is because in many cases they are not managing the money that they are currently earning properly. It's not how much you make it's how much you keep and how you make it work for you. Many people have learned the bad habit of living beyond their means. What I mean by this is maybe you're making $50,000 a year but your spending $60,000. That's only the beginning of the horror story for most people. In order to sustain this financial negative lifestyle they start to abuse their credit cards by using them to pay for debt. Before you know it they are thousands of dollars in debt with high interest rates on credit cards and loans.

Have you ever wondered how someone can become a multimillionaire and then end up broke? Many people believe that if you become a millionaire you are financially set for life. That is the furthest thing from the truth. Majority of professional athletes go broke only a few years after they retire. Over 90% of people who win the lottery go broke within a short period of time, many worse off than before they won the lottery. It all comes down to money management and living within your means.

Also it's very important to grow your level of thinking as well. I believe the reason most people who come into a windfall of cash lose it so quickly is because they still have the same mindset as they did before the big money. Can you imagine having a $50,000 a year mindset and being thrust into

the lifestyle of a million? This is a recipe for disaster if you ask me. I don't believe in just living within your means. I believe in living life abundantly as well. living within your means is intelligent because it puts you in a position to increase your means. You will need extra money in order to do this.

Click here to check out the rest of (MONEY MANAGEMENT TIPS) on Amazon.

Check Out My Other Books

Below you'll find some of my other popular books that are popular on Amazon and Kindle as well. Simply click on the links below to check them out.

My Other Book – HOW TO START A BUSINESS FROM HOME

My Other Book – MAKE MONEY ONLINE

My Other Book – 10 WAYS TO GET OUT OF DEBT AND STAY OUT OF DEBT

My Other Book – FRUGAL LIVING

www.ingramcontent.com/pod-product-compliance
Lightning Source LLC
Chambersburg PA
CBHW081314180526
45170CB00007B/2702